HISTORY IN ART

ANCIENT CHINA

Raintree
Chicago, Illinois

DALE ANDERSON

© 2005 Raintree
Published by Raintree, a division of Reed Elsevier, Inc.
Chicago, Illinois
Customer Service 888-363-4266
Visit our website at www.raintreelibrary.com

For information, address the publisher:
Raintree, 100 N. LaSalle, Suite 1200, Chicago, IL 60602

Originated by Dot Gradations Ltd.
Printed and bound in China
by South China Printing Company.

09 08 07
10 9 8 7 6 5 4 3

Library of Congress Cataloging-in-Publication Data

Anderson, Dale, 1953-
   Ancient China / Dale Anderson.
      p. cm. -- (History in art)
   Includes index.
   ISBN 1-4109-0519-5 (lib. bdg.) — ISBN 1-4109-2037-2 (pbk.)
   ISBN 978-1-4109-0519-2(HC) — ISBN 978-1-4109-2037-9(pbk.)
   1. Art, Chinese--Juvenile literature. 2. China--Civilization--Juvenile literature. I. Title. II. Series.
   N7340.A556 2005
   709'.31--dc22
                                    2004007587

Acknowledgments
The publishers would like to thank the following for permission to reproduce photographs (t = top, b = bottom, l = left, r = right): AKG pp. 3 (Laurent Lecat), 15 (t), 16 (Laurent Lecat), 17 (Laurent Lecat), 19 (François Guenet), 35 (b); Art Archive pp. 20 (Bibliothèque Nationale Paris), 23 (t) (Genius of China Exhibition), 26, 27 (t) (Musée Cernuschi, Paris/Dagli Orti), 43 (b) (Dagli Orti); Bridgeman Art Library pp. 4 (Lauros/Giraudon), 5 (Musée Guimet, Paris), 6 (Archives Charmet), 9 (t) (Museum of Art & Far Eastern Antiquities, Ulricehamn), 9 (b) (Ashmolean Museum, Oxford), 10 (Museum of Fine Arts, Houston, Texas), 11 (b) (British Museum), 12 (Arthur M. Sackler, Harvard University Art Museums), 13 (Ashmolean Museum, Oxford), 14 (Irkutsk Museum), 15 (b) (Archives Charmet), 18 (Archives Charmet), 21 (b) (Paul Freeman), 22 (Giraudon), 24 (Lauros/Giraudon), 25 (t) (Arthur M. Sackler Museum, Harvard University Art Museums), 25 (b) (Lauros/ Giraudon), 27 (b), 29 (t), 29 (b) (Archives Charmet), 30 (Lauros/ Giraudon), 31, 32 (Musée Guimet, Paris), 33 (l) (Arthur M. Sackler Museum, Harvard University Art Museums), 34 (Lauros/Giraudon), 36 (Ashmolean Museum, Oxford), 38, 40 (Bibliothèque Nationale, Paris), 41 (Oriental Museum, Durham University), 44 (Museum of Art & Far Eastern Antiquities, Ulricehamn), 45 (Lauros/Giraudon); Corbis pp. 7 (Royal Ontario Museum), 28 (Charles & Josette Lenars), 35 (t) (Royal Ontario Museum), 37 (Royal Ontario Museum), 39 (Asian Art & Archaeology, Inc.), 42 (Pierre Colombel), 43 (t) (Christie's Images); Chris Fairclough p. 21 (t); Werner-Forman pp. 8, 11 (t) (British Museum), 23 (b), 33 (r).

Cover photograph of a Bodhisattva (Buddha-to-be) reproduced with permission of Werner Forman.

Every effort has been made to contact copyright holders of any material reproduced in this book. Any omissions will be rectified in subsequent printings if notice is given to the publishers.

The paper used to print this book comes from sustainable resources.

Contents

Art as Evidence

For many centuries, little was known about life in ancient China. However, in the last hundred years, **archaeologists** have dug up long-buried works of art. These objects—whether small pieces of metal or carved stone, or life-size human figures made of hardened clay—reveal much about how people lived in China thousands of years ago.

China's long history

China is one of the most ancient **civilizations**. Rulers in other parts of Asia tried to follow the example of China's wealthy, powerful emperors. The Chinese invented many useful products and created brilliant works of art. European merchants traveled vast distances to buy Chinese products, and made large profits selling them in their own countries. People in other Asian countries were also eager to obtain goods made in China. Many adopted Chinese culture, taking Chinese beliefs and practices and making them part of their own ways of life.

The story of China began about 10,000 years ago, and Chinese culture has continued to develop right up to our own time. This book focuses on ancient China, from around 5000 B.C.E. to the end of the first great Chinese **empire** in about 220 C.E. During this period, the people of China created many of the features that make their culture unique.

▼ This drum-shaped container dates from between 200 B.C.E. and 200 C.E., offering evidence of Chinese technology from this period.

The container held cowrie shells; these had been used as money in China in earlier centuries and were still placed in tombs.

The figures on top are spinning and weaving, showing that the Chinese had these technologies.

Bird figures decorate the bottom section.

Workers fashioned this container from bronze, a metal made by mixing copper and tin.

▶ This stone statue from 380–530 C.E. shows that a new religious belief had entered China by this time.

Clues to life in the past

We can learn much about ancient China from the art and **artifacts** that have been uncovered. The appearance of certain metals shows that the Chinese had developed techniques for mining and working with those metals. Some objects give clues about the structure of Chinese society, telling us that rulers and wealthy people enjoyed high status while the vast majority of people did not. Other works hint at religious beliefs. Still others give us glimpses of daily life.

Of course, art cannot answer every question about life in ancient China. Parts of some artifacts are missing, making it difficult to know exactly how the objects were used. Most fascinating to researchers are items that have unusual, possibly symbolic decorations. Historians continue to study these pieces, hoping to discover their meaning.

Proper names in China

In China, a person's family name comes first, followed by his or her given name. Most names are made up of three words (Chinese characters), and it is standard practice to join the second and third characters together—for example, Mao Zedong or Li Yanping. With important historical figures the word Zi ("tser") is added after the family name. An example would be the ancient writer Sun Zi ("swun tser"). Some ancient names of just two syllables are run together, as with the name of the ancient philosopher Laozi ("lao tser"). Chinese writing has no way of showing capitals, but they are usually used for Chinese names written in English.

The bump on top of the Buddha's head reflects Indian traditions. Many early Chinese statues of the Buddha also gave the figure elongated earlobes, another Indian tradition. Both are symbols of the Buddha's enlightenment.

The raised, open right hand is a traditional pose for the Buddha.

The statue portrays the Buddha, founder of Buddhism, a religion that originated in India.

Chinese Technologies

The Chinese were the inventors of gunpowder, a substance they used to make fireworks more than a thousand years ago. Not long after that, they discovered that a magnetic compass would always point north, creating a useful instrument for sailors trying to find their way at sea.

Making silk

Silk is a lightweight, easily stretched fabric made from the cocoons spun by silkworm caterpillars. The Chinese began making silk well before 2000 B.C.E. This was—and still is—a very difficult and time-consuming process. Workers had to care for and feed huge numbers of silkworms, because they needed 2,000 to produce about 1.1 pounds (0.5 kilograms) of silk. They had to watch the caterpillars to see when they were ready to lay their eggs—this is when they make their cocoons. To keep the caterpillars spinning, workers had to feed them leaves every few hours, all day and all night. (Silkworms eat only the leaves of certain trees: mainly mulberry, but in northern China, oak.)

After that, the cocoons had to be boiled so that the workers could untangle all the strands of silk. Then workers had to twist some strands together to make a tougher fiber that could be woven.

All the effort paid off. Silk became a highly valued fabric that only the wealthy could afford. Eventually, people in other lands heard about Chinese silk. A trade route opened up, connecting China with Europe, and merchants brought the beautiful fabric to ancient Rome. This route—called the **Silk Road**—was used for hundreds of years.

Some of the people in the crowd fly beautifully decorated kites; these were developed in China and spread from there to other lands.

The first Chinese kites were made of silk and controlled by long, fine silk threads; later kites were made of paper, another Chinese invention.

▶ This painting on cloth from the 1800s shows the ancient Chinese technology of gunpowder.

Here the powder is being used to make fireworks as part of a celebration.

Making paper

The Chinese developed a system of writing some time between 2000 and 1000 B.C.E. For centuries, they had written on silk, bamboo, and wood. However, each of these materials had disadvantages. Only the wealthy could afford books made of silk, while bamboo and wood were bulky and difficult to store and transport. Soon after 100 C.E., the Chinese began using a new writing surface—paper. The Chinese credit a government official named Cai Lun ("tseye loon") with inventing the new material. Within a few hundred years, it was being widely used across China.

Carving jade

Another ancient Chinese **technology** was developed for its beauty and its symbolic significance. As early as 5,000 years ago, the Chinese began making jade objects. Like silk making, this process requires great skill and patience. Jade comes from various stones, mainly jadeite and nephrite, and it is so hard that it cannot be cut. Therefore, the Chinese had to grind the stone using sand mixed with water. Since this process took a long time, the Chinese valued jade very highly. Jade is also very long-lasting. For this reason, the Chinese saw it as a symbol of immortal life, and often placed jade objects in people's tombs. Many of these objects can still be seen.

▶ This jade object dates from 300 to 200 B.C.E., when the Chinese had already been carving jade for thousands of years.

Because it is durable and long-lasting, jade was considered a symbol of immortal life, so many jade objects were placed in tombs.

The object was the scabbard for a sword.

The patterns on the scabbard suggest the limbs of a tree, with a monkey.

The Story of Ancient China

Geography shaped the development of ancient China. The first Chinese communities arose in river valleys with rich soil that could support farming. Northwest China became the birthplace of Chinese **civilization** and eventually the seat of kingdoms and **empires**.

Land and rivers

Two great rivers drain eastern China, flowing west to east until they reach the China Sea. To the north is the Huang He ("hwang her"). As it moves east, it picks up some of the rich yellow soil of northern China, thus earning its name (Huang He translates as "Yellow River"). To the south is China's other great river, the Yangzi ("yang zer"), known to the Chinese as the "Long River."

The rivers, especially the Huang He, sometimes overflow. Since the land in this region is low and flat, the floodwaters can cover huge areas and devastate farms and villages.

Farming begins

By 8000 B.C.E., people living along both rivers were farming. Those who lived along the Huang He grew millet, a grain well suited to the cooler, drier climate of this region. They raised sheep and cattle as well. To the south, the warmer, wetter climate was perfect for growing rice, a grain that became the chief crop along the Yangzi. People in this area raised cattle and water buffalo. Those in both regions also tamed dogs and farmed pigs and chickens.

▼ This ink painting on silk, dating from around 1100 C.E., is thought to show a city along the Huang He.

Workers carry on their trades beside the river, making products that can be shipped to other parts of China.

Boats ply the river, providing an easy way of transporting goods and people across China.

The bustling city is built on both sides of the river.

Different styles of pottery

The roots of Chinese civilization were planted along the banks of the Huang He, around 10,000–8000 B.C.E. Pottery from these early times gives important clues to how the people lived. Burials are also helpful because everyday objects were placed in graves, apparently to make things easier for the dead person in the world of spirits.

Pottery of the Yangshao culture (5000–3000 B.C.E.) was made by coiling. Potters began by shaping the wet clay into long snakelike pieces. Starting at the bottom, they then wound the coils on top of each other until they had made a pot or a bowl. They used a flat tool to smooth the edges of the coils on the outside. Inside, however, the outline of each coil can still be seen.

The Longshan culture came in 3000–2200 B.C.E. This culture developed the potter's wheel, a round, flat surface connected to a spinning mechanism. The potter throws a lump of clay onto the wheel and shapes an object while turning the wheel. Its spinning allows the potter to make objects with thinner sides and more complex shapes than is possible with coiling.

▶ This pottery urn is about 5,000 years old. The Chinese had already been making pottery for thousands of years before the urn was created.

This piece shows the style of pottery in western China, where simple jars and urns were decorated with black and red designs; Eastern Chinese potters used more complex designs and did not usually paint their pots.

▶ This piece is the lid from a pot that reflects the Yangshao style. The face might be that of a shaman, or religious leader.

Firing pottery

Pottery is first shaped and then **fired** in an oven called a kiln. The firing hardens the clay so that it keeps its shape. Firing pottery makes the pieces stronger and longer lasting. Ordinary clay is eventually broken down by water, but if the fire in the oven reaches 932 °F (500 °C), pottery can hold water and keep its shape.

This kind of pottery is similar to the simple earthenware used for traditional clay flower pots; its reddish base comes from the color of the clay used to make the pot.

The coils on the outside were smoothed before the pot was fired.

The Shang Dynasty

By around 2000 B.C.E., northern China had many different cultures. Within a few hundred years, one of them gained control of a wider area. That culture gave birth to the Shang ("shahng") **Dynasty**, the first Chinese government to leave written records. Shang rulers controlled a large area of northeastern China from about 1600 to 1050 B.C.E. The Shang culture influenced even areas they did not rule, and many practices established during the Shang period were followed by later Chinese rulers.

Forging a kingdom

Several technologies helped the Shang conquer neighboring lands. Bronze weapons gave them advantages over groups still using stone weapons.

The Shang also mastered horsemanship and, later, chariots, giving their armies added speed and power.

Shang rulers controlled many elements of society. The bronze industry produced magnificent works, some weighing over 990 pounds (450 kilograms). This output could only be achieved by firm government direction of the workers who mined, melted, and **cast** the metal.

Another important **technology** was writing. The Shang were not the first Chinese people to have writing, but they improved the writing system.

▼ Shang ritual bronzes were made in an amazing variety of shapes and sizes.

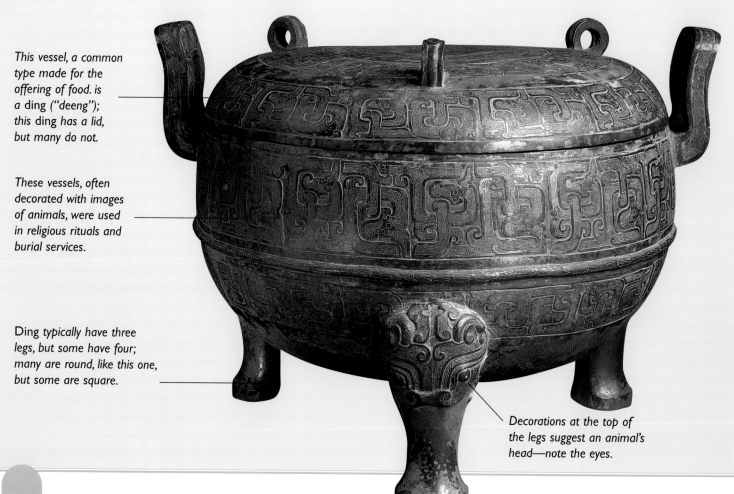

This vessel, a common type made for the offering of food. is a ding ("deeng"); this ding has a lid, but many do not.

These vessels, often decorated with images of animals, were used in religious rituals and burial services.

Ding *typically have three legs, but some have four; many are round, like this one, but some are square.*

Decorations at the top of the legs suggest an animal's head—note the eyes.

▶ When making bronze, the Chinese included some lead, copper, and tin. This allowed them to make sharper points, useful for weapons like this axe.

Large ceremonial axes like this one are linked to military authority and royal power—this axe was found in a tomb belonging to a person who was probably of high rank.

There is some evidence that axes like this one were used in executions.

An ancestor cult

To reinforce their power, Shang kings made themselves the center of a state religion. They claimed to communicate with their dead ancestors, who were thought to be close to Shang Di ("dee"), the emperor of heaven. The king could contact his ancestors to learn Shang Di's wishes. He could also ask them to persuade Shang Di to help him and his people. The king kept his ancestors happy by making regular offerings of food and drink. He even sacrificed animals—and sometimes humans—to maintain peace with his ancestors and the gods. Carrying out **rituals** to please ancestors remained an important feature of Chinese society for thousands of years.

All Shang rulers were males. Only a brother or son of the ruler could become a king, because the Shang believed that only males could communicate with ancestors.

Vast tombs

Shang rulers demonstrated their power by building elaborate tombs. They put thousands to work digging huge holes up to 40 feet (12 meters) into the ground and constructing large burial chambers out of wood. Other workers spent months creating pottery, jade, bronze, and other objects that went into the tombs. Some servants even accompanied their rulers to death, volunteering—we do not know how freely—to die as well.

Oracle bones

To speak to their ancestors, Shang rulers used oracle bones. These were animal bones, most often the shoulder bone of an ox or the lower part of a turtle shell. When the king asked his ancestor a question, a priest pressed a hot poker into a spot on the bone. The way the bone cracked determined whether the answer was yes or no. On many of these bones, the priest wrote down the question and then the answer.

▶ This oracle bone dates from about 1500 B.C.E. The earliest known examples of Chinese writing are found on bones like this one.

Bronze Casting

Shang bronzes show a high level of artistry and skill. The Shang made impressive bronze weapons, but their **ritual** vessels demonstrate their most dazzling abilities.

Casting techniques

The Chinese used two main methods for **casting** bronze—piece-mold and lost-wax. The Shang relied on the piece-mold method. They began by making a model of the object they wanted to create. Then they pressed soft clay all around the model, inside and out, in order to get an impression of every surface area. Once the clay was dry, they carefully cut it away from the model. The result was a reverse copy of the desired shape.

Once ready, the clay was **fired** in an oven like any piece of pottery. The pieces were then put together in a frame and hot, liquid bronze was poured in. When the bronze cooled, the workers could take the mold away, leaving the bronze object they wanted.

One reason the Shang used the piece-mold method was that it enabled them to **mass-produce** bronzes.

The pottery molds could be used more than once. Many Shang bronzes were made by first casting pieces that stuck out from the main body of the vessel—such as legs or handles—and then adding the body.

The other method, the lost-wax process, was used more in later periods of Chinese history. With this technique, workers made a wax model of the desired object. They then covered the wax model with clay to make a shell that followed the model's shape. Firing the pottery melted the wax and left a space into which liquid bronze was poured. The liquid filled the space and, when it cooled and hardened, created the desired bronze. The pottery pieces were cut away and the bronze vessel remained.

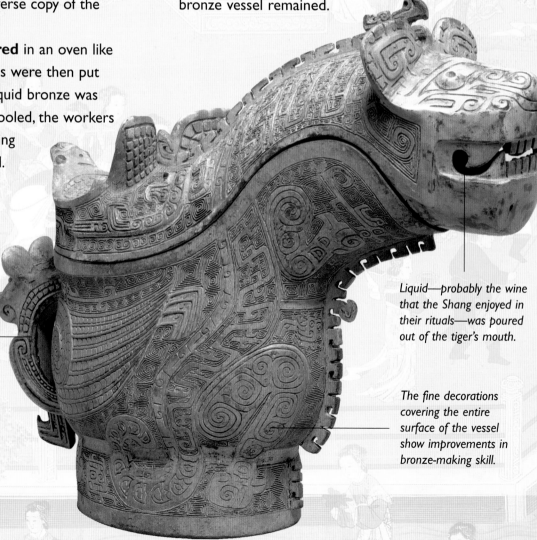

Tigers were not the only animals used to decorate these vessels—others take the shapes of elephants, rhinoceroses, sheep, and oxen.

▶ This pitcher-shaped ritual vessel was made in the 1200s B.C.E.

Liquid—probably the wine that the Shang enjoyed in their rituals—was poured out of the tiger's mouth.

The fine decorations covering the entire surface of the vessel show improvements in bronze-making skill.

Mirrors were often placed in tombs because they were thought to give off light, helping the spirit of the dead person by providing it with light for all eternity.

The stylized animal shapes are dragons, symbolizing good luck for the Chinese. These decorations appeared on the back of the bronze mirror, and the other side was polished so much that it could reflect what faced it—the ancient Chinese did not know how to make glass.

▶ This bronze mirror dates from the Warring States period (403–221 B.C.E.).

Ritual bronzes

Shang rituals included offerings of wine and food, so they needed several different types of vessels. Some pots were used for cooking. Other large vessels held wine to be poured into smaller goblets.

Many different bronze designs were created for these rituals, some of them echoing earlier forms. For instance, pots on tripods were similar to three-legged pottery pieces made centuries before. Four-legged pots might have been reserved for members of the royal family. Others were far more elaborate, using animal

heads and bodies or mixing several animal figures. Often they chose wild animals, rather than tame ones.

Many Shang bronzes were decorated with a face called a *taotie* ("tah-oh-tee-ay"). Historians disagree on whether this type of face was intended to be a monster to frighten evil spirits, a dragon to bring good fortune, an echo of a design used in past cultures, or an abstract design that did not represent anything at all. Whatever the meaning of the *taotie*, it was used frequently.

The Zhou Dynasty

Shang armies often fought against neighboring peoples, such as the Zhou ("joh") who lived in a kingdom to the west. Eventually, a Zhou king conquered the Shang. Zhou kings then led the most powerful state in northern China for the next few hundred years.

A new dynasty

The Zhou rulers developed a theory of government that became very important to Chinese **civilization**. They had long worshiped the god called Heaven, and the Zhou king was praised as the "Son of Heaven." The Zhou claimed that Heaven allowed a king to rule only as long as he was good to his people. If he did not rule well, Heaven would take the kingdom from him.

The Zhou used this theory to justify their conquest of the Shang. They charged Shang rulers with being corrupt and cruel. Because the Shang were tyrants, Heaven had allowed them to fall. This idea came to be called the **Mandate of Heaven**. It remained an important part of Chinese political thinking for nearly 3,000 years.

▶ The round, low shape and handles identify this vessel as a common type called a *gui* ("gooee").

*Some **ritual** vessels had inscriptions on the inside, intended to be read by the dead ancestors as they ate the food offered to them in sacrifice.*

*The base is made of **cast** bronze, but the lid of the gui is wooden—an unusual combination of materials.*

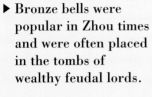

▶ Bronze bells were popular in Zhou times and were often placed in the tombs of wealthy feudal lords.

Bells were hung at an angle, allowing the player to hit them more accurately.

An inscription on each bell states what tones it makes.

The bells' almond shape allows each one to produce two different tones, depending on whether it is struck in the center or to the side.

Shaping society

The Zhou changed Chinese society, creating a class of wealthy landowners and giving large gifts of land to members of their families and to trusted officials. Those who received these gifts were also in charge of the thousands of peasants who lived on the land. When the landowners and officials died, the land and peasants were passed on to their sons.

The result was a **feudal system**, with the wealthy landowners dominating society. The king was at the top. Beneath him were the nobles who owned the land. Next came the officials who ran the government or managed the nobles' lands. At the bottom were the farmers.

The Western Zhou and the Eastern Zhou

Zhou rulers could not maintain peace and order. By the late 700s B.C.E., a revolt resulted in the death of the Zhou king. His son fled east, building a new capital. This marked a break between what is called the Western Zhou—the earliest period of Zhou rule—and the Eastern Zhou. By around 400 B.C.E., however, conflict erupted again and continued for most of the next two centuries.

◀ This painting on silk shows Emperor Yang Ti (581–618), who ruled during the Sui dynasty. It is one of many similar paintings from a history of China published in the 1400s.

China's dynasties

During its long history, China has been governed by several major **dynasties**. While some ruled for brief periods only, others led the country for several centuries. For over 3,500 years, the king—and later the emperor—had firm central control over Chinese society.

1600–1050 B.C.E.	– Shang Dynasty
1050–256	– Zhou ("joh") Dynasty
221–206	– Qin ("chin") Dynasty
206 B.C.E.–220 C.E.	– Han Dynasty
220–589	– Six Dynasties period
581–618	– Sui ("sway") Dynasty
618–907	– Tang ("tahng") Dynasty
907–960	– Five Dynasties Period
960–1279	– Song ("soong") Dynasty
1280–1368	– Yuan ("yoo-en") Dynasty
1368–1644	– Ming Dynasty
1644–1912	– Qing ("ching") Dynasty

The Qin Dynasty

From 403 to 221 B.C.E., Zhou China fell into an era called the Warring States period. For nearly 200 years, rival rulers built large armies and fought to gain control over each other's lands.

The First Emperor

In the 200s B.C.E., Zheng ("juhng"), the king of Qin ("chin"), gained the upper hand. He used military skill, bribery, and spying to conquer the other kingdoms and create China's first **empire**. He renamed himself Qin Shi Huangdi ("chin sher hwang-dee"), meaning "First Emperor of Qin."

The first emperor took many steps to unite the different kingdoms. For instance, he forced people across China to use the same weights and measures, the same coins, and the same system of writing. Government officials were sent throughout his lands to make sure that his laws were obeyed.

▼ This pottery figure was found in Qin Shi Huangdi's tomb. His special cap shows that he was an officer. Other officers had chest ribbons as well.

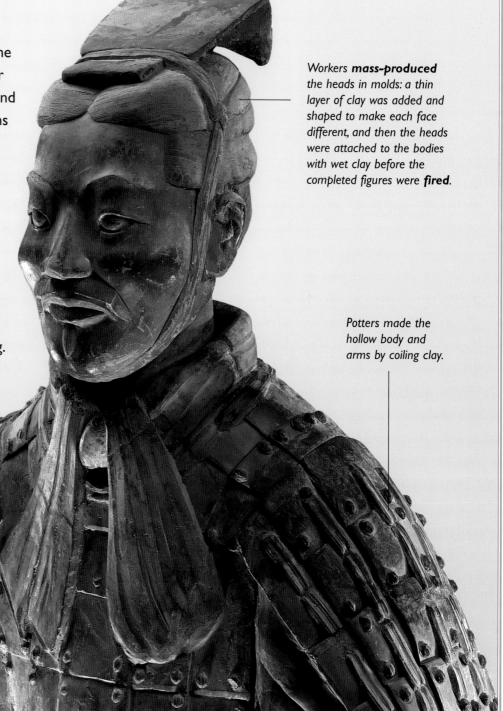

Workers **mass-produced** the heads in molds: a thin layer of clay was added and shaped to make each face different, and then the heads were attached to the bodies with wet clay before the completed figures were **fired**.

Potters made the hollow body and arms by coiling clay.

Like other officers, he wears armor over cloth tunics.

A buried army

Qin Shi Huangdi also compelled people to work on large building projects—one of these was a massive tomb complex for himself. The riches placed in this tomb have yet to be uncovered. However, scientists have made impressive finds by digging in areas around the central burial mound. In the 1970s, they found more than 7,000 life-size soldiers and horses made of terra cotta (a kind of pottery). Pottery sculpture of human figures was rare in China before Qin Shi Huangdi's tomb.

The tomb reveals that Qin Shi Huangdi had vast wealth and complete control of his people. Building the tomb and making the objects placed in it took a small army of workers many years. The soldiers held thousands of bronze weapons—meaning that these were no longer available to real armies. Dozens of working chariots were also buried in the tomb.

Qin Shi Huangdi vowed that his empire would last thousands of years. Instead, it ended shortly after his death. Still, Qin Shi Huangdi had a lasting impact. He unified several kingdoms into a single empire with a strong central government.

Qin Shi Huangdi

The first emperor was a teenager when he became king of Qin, though at first an adult ran the kingdom for him. Soon after taking full power in 238 B.C.E., he put down a rebellion, killed one high court official, and sent another into exile. He ruled harshly, killing anyone who stood in his way. When scholars complained about his actions, he had more than four hundred of them killed and gave orders that many of their books should be burned. Having survived several assassination attempts, he sent out an expedition in search of a liquid that he thought would give him eternal life. When that search failed, he brought magicians to his court in the hope that they could help him live forever. He took personal control of all areas of government and became known as a cruel but skilled emperor.

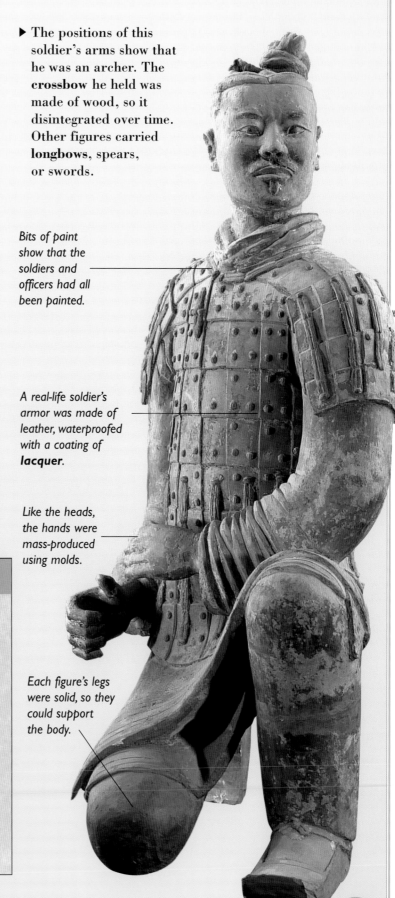

▶ The positions of this soldier's arms show that he was an archer. The **crossbow** he held was made of wood, so it disintegrated over time. Other figures carried **longbows**, spears, or swords.

Bits of paint show that the soldiers and officers had all been painted.

A real-life soldier's armor was made of leather, waterproofed with a coating of **lacquer**.

Like the heads, the hands were mass-produced using molds.

Each figure's legs were solid, so they could support the body.

The Han Dynasty

When Qin Shi Huangdi died, one of his sons took the throne. Then a younger son killed this brother and seized power for himself. For the next four years, conflict raged across northern China as different leaders tried to gain control and the young emperor fought back.

▼ This silk painting from the 1600s C.E. shows how a later artist imagined the Han emperor Wudi leaving his palace.

A new ruler

The victor was Liu Bang, who had been born a peasant and served as a police officer in Qin times. Liu joined in the rebellion against the emperor under Xiang Yu, the man who defeated the Qin ruler. Given control of a region of western China as a reward, he soon revolted against Xiang Yu. In 206 B.C.E., he gained the throne, proclaimed himself emperor, and took the name Gaozu ("gao-zoo").

Wudi was much respected for expanding China's reach to new lands and for bringing scholars learned in the works of Confucius into the government.

The interest in Wudi shown by an artist who lived more than 1,700 years later reveals the reverence that many Chinese had for the Han rulers.

A lasting empire

Gaozu's reign launched the Han **dynasty**, and it ruled China for the next 400 years. This period was generally peaceful and prosperous. Han emperors introduced a system of **imperial** government (the strong central control of a realm that includes many different peoples) that later dynasties followed. In fact, Han rule was so important in shaping Chinese culture that even today Chinese people call themselves "children of the Han."

The emperor Wudi ("woo-dee"), who reigned from 141 to 87 B.C.E., sent out armies to expand China's territory. Qin conquests had brought the Yangzi River valley into the **empire**. Wudi's victories now brought regions farther west and farther south under imperial rule for the first time.

Still, Han rule was not all glorious and peaceful. This was partly because Han emperors had many wives and many sons. Struggles for power often took place when powerful sons (and their powerful mothers) refused to accept the heir named by the emperor. Another problem arose when children gained the throne at a young age. **Regents** ruled for them until they reached adulthood.

However, regents were not always willing to give up power. One, called Wang Mang ("wahng mahng"), actually made himself emperor and declared a new dynasty. However, he held the throne only from 9 to 23 C.E., when he was overthrown by a member of the Liu family, who restored Han rule.

▼ These pottery horses and men date from early Han times.

Artists spent the most time working on the head and face for each figure; here, the horse's head is modeled in vivid detail.

These horses do not have saddles and bridles—other pieces show that such riding gear was used in early Han times.

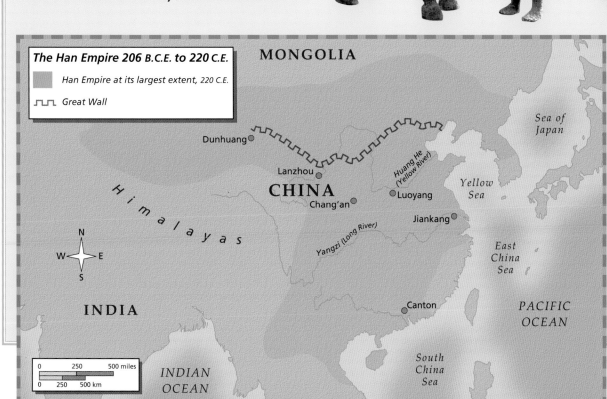

Traces of paint indicate that the pieces had been painted.

The Han Empire 206 B.C.E. to 220 C.E.

Han Empire at its largest extent, 220 C.E.

┌┴┐ Great Wall

MONGOLIA

Dunhuang

Lanzhou

CHINA

Chang'an

Huang He (Yellow River)

Luoyang

Yellow Sea

Sea of Japan

Jiankang

East China Sea

H i m a l a y a s

Yangzi (Long River)

Canton

PACIFIC OCEAN

INDIA

South China Sea

N
W E
S

0   250   500 miles
0   250   500 km

INDIAN OCEAN

◄ Han China governed a larger area than any previous Chinese state, even gaining control of present-day northern Korea and northern Vietnam.

19

Imperial Government

The Qin and Han rulers introduced strong central government to China. The Han rulers who followed Qin Shi Huangdi were just as committed to maintaining **imperial** rule, but they aimed to win the people's loyalty rather than force their obedience.

The Qin system

Qin Shi Huangdi's **philosophy**, legalism, held that rulers should pass tough laws and keep tight control over all aspects of government. The first emperor therefore imposed harsh taxes and labor demands on the peasants. He also broke the power of the feudal nobles, ordering them to leave their lands and move to his capital Xianyang ("zhan-yahng"), near the modern city of Xian. In their place, he sent officials to manage each part of the **empire**.

Each of the 36 districts was led by four officials. Two ran the local government, and the third headed the district army. The fourth directed a team of inspectors who watched all the government administrators in the district. These inspectors reported directly to the emperor about any administrators who disobeyed orders, took bribes, or performed wrongly in other ways.

▼ This painting from a later period portrays the emperor Qin Shi Huangdi's attack on scholars when they opposed his legalist rule.

The emperor Qin Shi Huangdi, seated on his throne, dispenses harsh justice to scholars who disagree with his policies.

One scholar pleads, probably for the lives of all his fellows and not just his own.

Here, scholars are being executed by being thrown into a pit.

Here books are burning—Qin Shi Huangdi ordered the burning of hundreds of texts, though some were later written again by scholars who had memorized them.

▶ The Great Wall of China that people see today was actually built around 1500 C.E., many centuries after its first construction.

The Great Wall

Qin Shi Huangdi had started building the Great Wall by linking together walls built by the rulers of different kingdoms. Under Wudi, work began again in an effort to keep the Xiongnu from entering China. The wall also protected traders, helping to open up the **Silk Road** to the west. In Han times, the wall was made of packed dirt. Later **dynasties** rebuilt it of brick and stone, and extended it to about 4,500 miles (7,300 kilometers). Much of this later structure still stands today.

Winning the people's allegiance

When Gaozu, the first Han ruler, gained the throne, he tried to win the allegiance of a people weary of high taxes and strong government. The toughest laws were overturned, and taxes were lowered. However, the emperor remained central to government, and the government was still the dominant force in Chinese society. Gaozu's chief minister began building the new emperor a huge palace even before control of the empire was secured. Gaozu objected but gave in when the minister reminded him that the Son of Heaven must "dwell in magnificent quarters" so he can "display his authority."

Protecting the people

Attacks from **nomads** in central Asia and Mongolia troubled Han China. Wudi managed to reduce the threat from central Asia, but the fierce Xiongnu ("shee-ung-nu") people to the north remained. In order to defend his empire against these powerful warriors, Wudi continued work on the Great Wall of China.

Wudi's structure was not simply a wall. It was a position defended at all times by soldiers who could respond to any threat. Every 6 miles (10 kilometers) or so, there was a watchtower, and every 18 miles (30 kilometers), there was a fort.

▼ This pottery model of a military watchtower dates from later Han times.

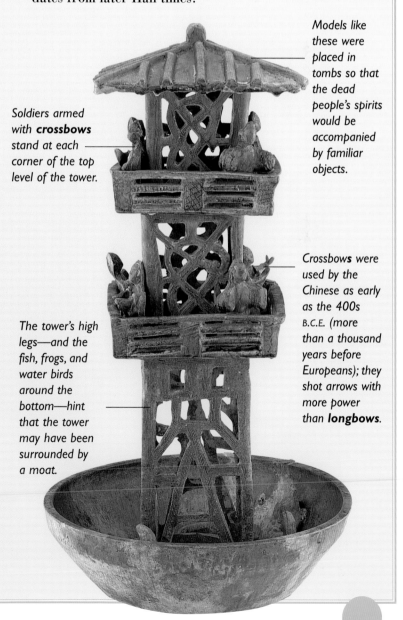

Models like these were placed in tombs so that the dead people's spirits would be accompanied by familiar objects.

Soldiers armed with **crossbows** stand at each corner of the top level of the tower.

Crossbows were used by the Chinese as early as the 400s B.C.E. (more than a thousand years before Europeans); they shot arrows with more power than **longbows**.

The tower's high legs—and the fish, frogs, and water birds around the bottom—hint that the tower may have been surrounded by a moat.

Conquest and Rule

Two groups were essential to the workings of the ancient Chinese **empire**—government officials and the army. The government officials played a vital role in creating and maintaining Han rule. The Han also needed huge armies to make their conquests and fight the **nomads**. Wudi sent out several expeditions of more than 100,000 troops against the Xiongnu in the north.

The army

All men between the ages of 23 and 56 were supposed to spend a month in military training after completing the harvest. However, over time, Chinese armies developed into professional military forces with clear ranks and different types of units—archers, spear-carrying infantry, a chariot force, and **cavalry**. These more professional soldiers wore leather armor and used bronze spears and swords, **crossbows** and **longbows**, and chariots. In Han times, iron weapons became more widespread.

The Han improved their cavalry in order to triumph over the horse-riding nomads. An official found a breed of big, strong, fast horses in the kingdom of Ferghana, in what is now eastern Uzbekistan. The Han called this breed "Heavenly Horses." These animals were a perfect replacement for the smaller horses the Chinese had. When Ferghana refused to sell the horses, Wudi sent an expedition to capture a few thousand animals and bring them back east. There, the government set up horse farms to breed more.

▶ This bronze of a "Heavenly Horse" from the 100s C.E. was found in a tomb.

With its raised legs and flowing tail, the horse embodies speed and power.

The only hoof touching the ground rests on a swallow, making the horse appear to be running so fast that it is flying.

Officials often rode in two-wheeled chariots with silk umbrellas to protect them from the sun.

▶ These bronze figures of a scholar-official and an attendant were placed in a government official's tomb sometime in the 100s C.E.

Attendants always had to be ready to carry out whatever task the official required them to perform.

Other similar pieces show soldiers carrying spears to protect officials from any danger.

A need for officials

In running their empire, the Han placed great emphasis on knowledge and education. Gaozu decided to staff the government with highly educated men, and Wudi went further. He declared that government officials had to learn the most important books of Confucian thinking (see page 40). He even created a university to train candidates. These scholar-officials became the main force in the **civil service**. Later on, the government used special examinations to fill many government posts.

In theory, the civil service was open to anyone. But only the wealthiest families could afford the many years of education children needed to learn the Confucian texts.

▼Engravings show Chinese characters used in the 700s C.E. Compare them to the writing on the oracle bone shown on page 11.

神會 備 以 將 堪 秉 窫 寔 薦 百 皇
徂宗 益 玉 迥 元 穎 极 不 跑 告 卒 十 帝
至大 塞 泉 報 降 凡 建 之 告 弗 一 元
尚真 武 禮 功 霊 大 田 句 于 嗣 月 年
饗皇 表 武 娶 惟 志 苦 地 建 未 天 己
帝 盎 載 品 敬 式 寒 豊 丰 式 資 盧 百 朔 子 朔 十

Chinese writing

Chinese writing uses symbols called "characters." Unlike the Western alphabet, with letters that stand for sounds, Chinese characters stand for ideas. This system had some advantages. For instance, it could be adopted for other languages because the way a word was pronounced did not matter. As a result, both Japan and Korea borrowed heavily from China's writing system when they created their own. Also, scholars could easily read texts written hundreds of years earlier, even if they spoke a language different from the one the text was written in. However, the system also had a big disadvantage: Chinese has thousands of characters and it takes many years to learn them all. Scholars were highly respected in ancient China, partly because of their mastery of this difficult writing system.

The Outside World

In Han times, the Chinese began to have more contact with the outside world. Conquests in what is now Korea and Vietnam began the spread of Chinese culture to those lands. For China, however, the most important connection was with central Asia—the source of the Heavenly Horses and other influences. Their great trading route, the **Silk Road**, also crossed central Asia.

Nomadic tribes

Han China was not always in conflict with its nomadic neighbors. Even the fierce Xiongnu became peaceful, though they remained a threat. By about 55 B.C.E., a Xiongnu leader agreed that his territory would be a tributary state. This meant that he had to pay a **tribute** (a certain amount paid on a regular basis) to the Chinese court. He also had to send a prince from his family to live in the court. Though treated well and educated in Chinese ways, the Xiongnu prince was really a hostage who could be punished if his father rebelled.

The Chinese regularly sent gifts—usually silk—to the **nomads**, who agreed to remain peaceful. This practice benefited the nomads, who traded most of this silk farther to the south and west. For the Chinese, the silk gifts were expensive (costing nearly 10 percent of the government's income), but the emperor was willing to pay a high price for peace.

▶ This bronze piece shows two tigers attacking a wild boar.

Artists of central Asia often depicted animals in conflict, not a common theme in Chinese art before this period.

The piece dates from Han times, reflecting China's expansion to the west and the increasing contact with the nomads of central Asia.

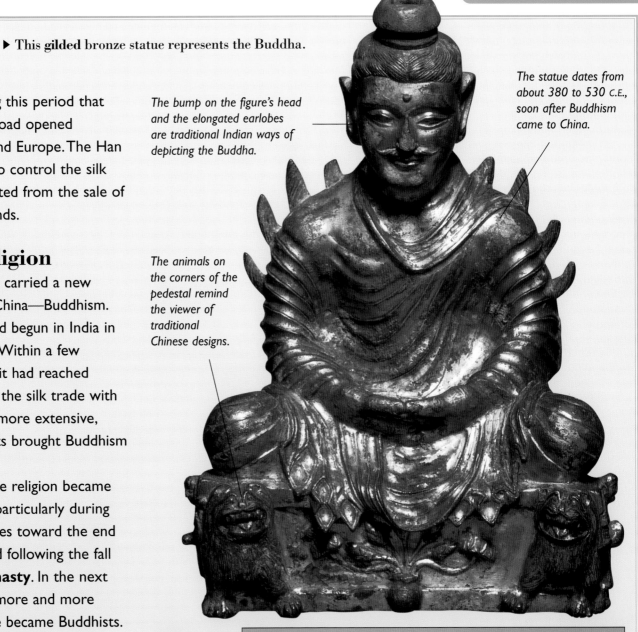

▶ This **gilded** bronze statue represents the Buddha.

The bump on the figure's head and the elongated earlobes are traditional Indian ways of depicting the Buddha.

The statue dates from about 380 to 530 C.E., soon after Buddhism came to China.

The animals on the corners of the pedestal remind the viewer of traditional Chinese designs.

It was during this period that the great Silk Road opened between Asia and Europe. The Han Chinese tried to control the silk trade, and profited from the sale of silk to other lands.

A new religion

Increased trade carried a new influence into China—Buddhism. This religion had begun in India in the 400s B.C.E. Within a few hundred years, it had reached central Asia. As the silk trade with China became more extensive, Asian merchants brought Buddhism into China.

Gradually, the religion became more popular, particularly during the difficult times toward the end of Han rule and following the fall of the Han **dynasty**. In the next few centuries, more and more Chinese people became Buddhists. By around 500 C.E., China had more than 10,000 Buddhist temples and nearly 160,000 Buddhist monks.

▶ This painted terra-cotta figure shows a rider from early Han times, before the Chinese had adopted the stirrup.

Stirrups

Contact with **nomads** brought new technologies to China. The chariot had come from central Asia about a thousand years before the Han rose to power. Later, in Han times, the stirrup arrived. A stirrup makes it easier to get on a horse and gives riders a firmer grip. The earliest Chinese images of stirrups do not show riders with their feet inside these devices. At first the Chinese probably used the new equipment only for getting onto their horses. However, later images do show riders with their feet firmly inside the stirrups.

25

Daily Life in Ancient China

Ancient Chinese society was based on farming. Although farmers were valued for their ability to produce food, they were treated badly. In Zhou times, they were subject to the feudal lords. After the Qin and Han **empires** broke the power of these nobles, farmers were supposedly free. But they still lived difficult lives, often on the edge of poverty.

▼ This pottery model of part of a farm was made during the Han period.

Making the land fruitful

Only about 20 percent of China's land area could be used for agriculture—the rest was too dry, hilly, or mountainous. Nevertheless, farmers managed to grow the required crops. New lands were settled, and **irrigation** projects brought water to areas that needed it. New types of plows were invented, allowing the farmers to plow deeper into the ground. The government taught them to keep the soil healthy by planting a series of different crops, because the soil would lose its nutrients if the same one were planted all the time. Many waste products, including human waste, were spread on the fields to fertilize the crops.

Some Chinese kept sheep, using them for their wool; other animals farmers had domesticated included chickens and dogs.

Farmers' lives

Farmers lived in small villages of about a hundred homes. Their farms tended to be small, since Han inheritance laws required landowners to divide their land among all their sons when they died. According to official written records from Han times, farm families averaged three children.

Farmers worked hard throughout the year. Chao Cuo ("chah-oh coo-oh"), writing in 178 B.C.E., noted, "They labor at plowing in the spring and hoeing in the summer, harvesting in the autumn and storing foodstuff in winter." Though animals pulled the plows, much farm work was done by hand. In addition to tending their farms and doing a month of military service, all men had to work for the government one month in each year. In this way, the farmers were used to build palaces and tombs, create irrigation ditches, and provide the workforce for government-run industries.

Then there were taxes. Han taxes were not as high as those under Qin rule. Farmers had to give only 3 percent of their autumn crops to the state. The government also took steps to help those whose farms were destroyed by floods and droughts. For many farmers, however, the combined pressures of work, forced labor, and taxes were simply too much. Many gave up their own land and offered to work for large landowners as tenant farmers.

▶ This barking dog from Han times has called to its master for about 2,000 years.

▼ This Han model shows a pig sty.

The farmer seems to be reaching into a basket or container, probably in order to feed the pig.

Steps lead to this upper ledge.

Pork and chicken were the chief meats eaten in ancient China, but meat was not a major part of the diet then.

Farm animals

The Chinese tamed many animals. Pigs, cattle, and chickens were raised for food. In the north, Han farmers began to use oxen to pull plows and do other farm work. In the south, water buffalo were used to perform the same tasks. Dogs were put to work as well. Many pottery figures of dogs show them wearing harnesses. They were probably used to pull sleighs.

City Life

The first cities were centers for government and religion. In Zhou times, cities grew larger and became centers of industry and trade. By the Warring States period, one city, Linzi ("leen-zee"), in modern Shandong ("shahn-dohng") province, had a few hundred thousand people, living in 70,000 households. There were several capitals during Zhou times and two during the Han period, but no single capital in the Warring States period.

The cities

Cities were surrounded by walls made of packed dirt. To build these walls, two temporary vertical wooden supports were placed about 3–4 inches (8–10 centimeters) apart. Earth was packed between the two supports and stamped down to compact it. Then the wooden supports were taken away and repositioned next to this earthen wall to make the next section.

Work in cities

Life in the cities was exciting. People filled the streets to buy goods from craft workers and food sellers. Street entertainers performed for the crowds. However, the culture of ancient China generally valued the work of farmers more than the contribution made by the different groups of city people. Society was divided into four groups ranked according to

▶ This pottery statue shows a common figure in Chinese cities—the fishmonger. With many cities built along rivers, the Chinese often had fish available to them.

their value. Scholar-officials headed the list, followed by farmers. Next came craft workers, while merchants ranked at the bottom. Laws were passed to prevent merchants from wearing silk and riding in carriages. They were also barred from owning land or becoming officials. These laws were not always enforced, but they reveal the difficulties that merchants faced. Still, the merchants' work was vital to the Chinese economy, and some of them managed to prosper.

The fishmonger is standing to do his work—workers stood or knelt on the floor, since there were no chairs.

Fish was a major source of protein for the Chinese—they had no refrigeration, but some fish could be preserved by drying, or people would buy fresh fish on the day they wanted it.

Growing industries

Many new industries grew up in **imperial** times. The Chinese first began using iron during the Warring States period. Very early on, they made iron weapons and tools by **casting** them in molds, rather than by hammering them into shape. Europeans did not cast iron until many centuries later. In the Warring States period, iron makers became wealthy. The Han government prevented them from growing too powerful by taking over the iron trade. Although private owners continued to make the iron, the government controlled the buying and selling of iron goods. It also seized control of the salt industry and the grain trade. The government took these steps to replace revenue (income) lost by cutting taxes on farmers.

Acupuncture

Some city dwellers were doctors. Nearly 5,000 years ago, the Chinese developed a medical treatment—acupuncture—that is still used today. In this technique, extremely thin needles are inserted into the body. The Chinese believe that disease is caused by a lack of balance between the female force, *yin* ("yeen"), and the male force, *yang* ("yahng"). This lack of balance blocks the flow of the body's energy. Inserting the needles is supposed to restore the balance and allow the energy to flow freely.

▼ A carved ivory statue shows a doctor practicing acupuncture while the patient's family looks on.

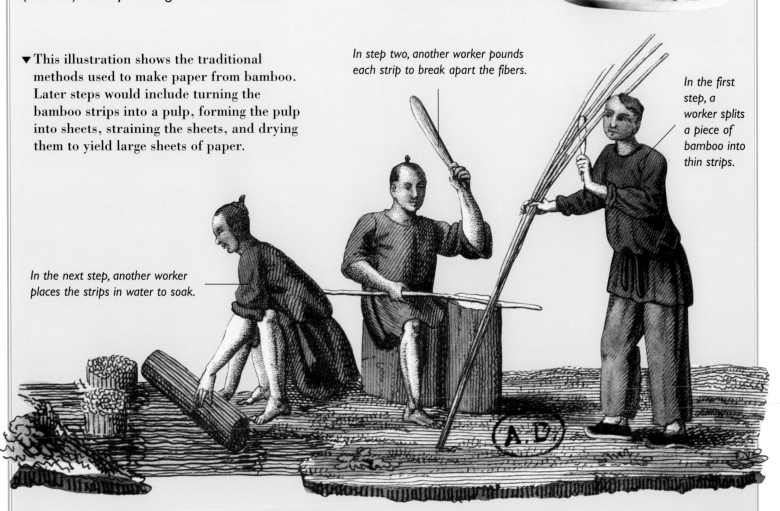

▼ This illustration shows the traditional methods used to make paper from bamboo. Later steps would include turning the bamboo strips into a pulp, forming the pulp into sheets, straining the sheets, and drying them to yield large sheets of paper.

In step two, another worker pounds each strip to break apart the fibers.

In the first step, a worker splits a piece of bamboo into thin strips.

In the next step, another worker places the strips in water to soak.

Architecture

We have discovered much about many ancient cultures from the stone or brick palaces and temples that they built. That is not true of ancient China. Although some brick and stone were used, most structures were made from wood and plaster, materials that are destroyed by time. Even the great palaces of the Qin and Han rulers have disappeared, since they were largely made of wood. Fortunately, pottery models placed in graves and wall decorations reveal many details about ancient Chinese architecture. Even the way the tombs themselves were built gives some useful information.

▶ This scene reveals some construction methods used in ancient China. Other models from the Han period show that homes were built in large courtyards, set off from the street by outer walls.

Houses

Buildings, including family homes, were built following the **post-and-lintel system** that was common throughout the ancient world. Using this method, vertical posts are sunk into the ground. These posts hold up a horizontal piece, the lintel. In multistory structures, the lintel must bear the weight of additional posts. On the top floor, the lintel supports the roof.

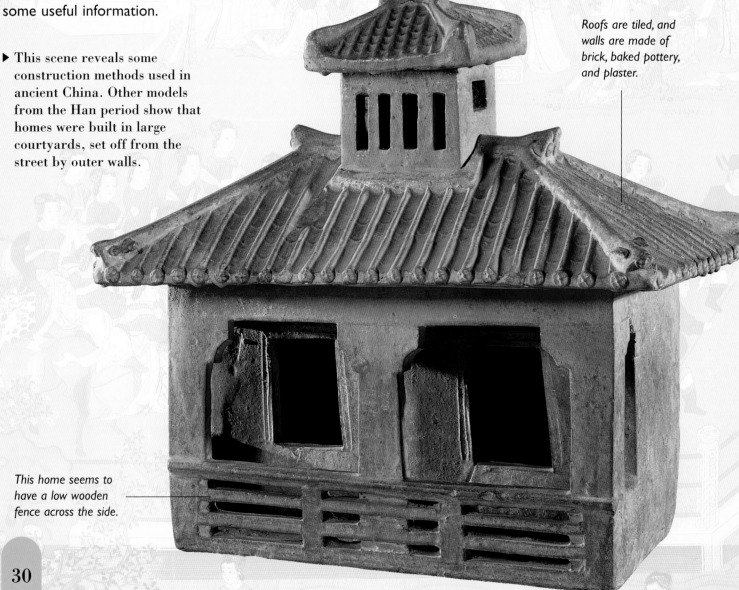

Roofs are tiled, and walls are made of brick, baked pottery, and plaster.

This home seems to have a low wooden fence across the side.

In ancient China, the posts and lintels were made of wood. Plaster and mud, bamboo screens, or clay filled the walls. Wood was chosen not just because it was practical but also because the Chinese thought that wood had special symbolic value. Wood came from living trees and was linked with life—a connection that made it desirable to have in a home. Wood could be damaged by moisture, however. To combat this, the Chinese built their homes on platforms. The higher the platform, the higher the status of the homeowner.

Outer walls enclosed an outer courtyard and then an inner one, where the house stood. Some homes had watchtowers where guards stood watch, in case of attack. The homes of wealthy people included a screen wall. This wall, made of wood, tile, or brick, stood near the entrance to the house. Visitors could stand behind it to adjust their clothing before entering.

In Zhou times, three generations of a family lived in one home. Grown sons and their families lived with their parents until the father died, and the oldest son inherited the land. Rooms in the house were allocated according to the person's status. The homeowner had the main room. Elderly members of the family lived in the back. Younger members lived to the side of the homeowner, with those of higher status on the left and others on the right.

Furnishings

The ancient Chinese did not have chairs. People knelt on straw mats on the floor. Beds and couches began to be used in the Warring States period. There were tables for eating and chests of drawers for storing goods. Wealthier people owned furniture that was more skillfully constructed and made of higher quality wood. The poor, however, could afford only the most basic furniture, such as tables for eating. They might even have had to make such items themselves. For lighting, the Chinese used oil lamps.

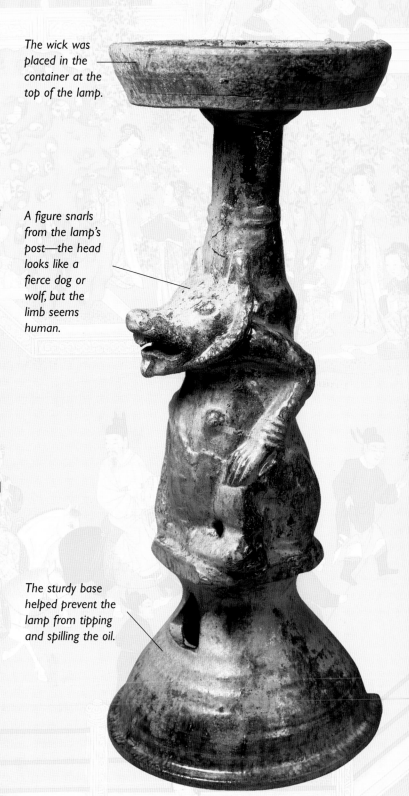

▼ Pottery lamps were typically used by the common people. Wealthier people had lamps made of bronze or **gilded** bronze.

The wick was placed in the container at the top of the lamp.

A figure snarls from the lamp's post—the head looks like a fierce dog or wolf, but the limb seems human.

The sturdy base helped prevent the lamp from tipping and spilling the oil.

31

Food

Han farmers had to work hard, partly because they had to support a growing population. In the year 2 C.E., the government took a **census** and found that there were nearly 60 million people living in Han lands (more than a quarter of all the people alive in the world at the time). However, this population was drastically reduced by the floods, droughts, and wars that marred later Han times.

Lacquerware was perfect for liquids because the lacquer coating made wood waterproof.

Eating

People mainly ate grains and vegetables. The chief grains were those most suited to China's geography, including millet and wheat in the north and rice in the south. Rice was especially valuable, because southern farmers could produce two harvests a year.

▼ This elegant cup was carved out of wood and then coated with lacquer. Some lacquer pieces cost more than bronzes.

The cup is in the form of a lotus blossom, a symbol of rebirth that was linked to Buddhism.

For many centuries, lacquered objects were only black, red, or both, but in Han times, the Chinese learned how to produce lacquer goods in other colors.

▼ The *yi* or *fangyi* was a rectangular vessel used to serve **ritual** wine.

The Chinese character used to write taotie *contains the character for "eat"—the* taotie *were thought to have huge appetites.*

This bronze dates from late Shang times in the 1100s B.C.E.

The face on the front shows a traditional motif called the taotie pattern.

The taotie *was thought to be a monster—scary eyes stare forth, appearing to threaten the observer.*

Most people's diets did not include much meat, at least in the times of the Qin and Han **dynasties**. In earlier periods, the Chinese had kept herds of cattle, sheep, and goats. However, as the population increased, more land was taken over for growing crops, and there was less land available for grazing. Oxen and water buffalo were still used to pull plows, but chickens and pigs were now the only animals raised for food. They

provided the main meat elements in the diet, while fish and soybeans provided additional protein.

The ancient Chinese did not think cow's milk was suitable to drink. They did drink tea, a practice that began some time before 2000 B.C.E. They also drank wine, although it was made from grain rather than grapes.

Chinese cooking aims for a balance of ingredients and flavors. These goals build on ancient ideas. Back in Shang times, a scholar wrote that cooks should seek to balance the five flavors—sweet, sour, bitter, spicy, and salty. He linked the foods that provided each of these flavors to different organs of the body and wrote that this balance would keep each organ in good condition and protect a person's health.

▼ The illustrations on these lacquered baskets show sons who were legendary for their obedience.

Lacquer

Lacquer is a varnish that comes from the sap of a tree native to China and now also grown in Japan. When the tree is ten years old, cuts are made in the trunk to collect the sap. Cutting the tree kills it, but the roots produce other trees that can be harvested in a few years. The tree is related to poison ivy, and the liquid sap can irritate the skin. The sap, a thick white or gray liquid, has to be strained, pounded, stirred, and heated to make it into lacquer. Once the lacquer has been applied to the surface of an object, it must be placed in moist air to dry. After it dries, the lacquer can be polished to produce a high shine. The coating not only forms a brilliant surface but also makes the object waterproof. It was therefore used to coat plates, bowls, and drinking vessels.

Entertainment

While peasants spent most of their time working, the wealthy could enjoy music, dancing, theater, and games. City dwellers, in particular, had several kinds of entertainment available to them.

Music and dancing

The Chinese were deeply interested in music. In fact, they used the same character to write the words "music" and "enjoyment." This interest extended so far that the Han created a government office charged with collecting traditional and folk songs. Instruments included drums, bells, flutes with several pipes, and stringed instruments like the *qin* ("chin"), a kind of **zither**.

Dancing dates back to the earliest Chinese cultures. Pottery figures from around 3000 B.C.E. show groups of people dancing. In the Shang and Zhou **dynasties**, people danced with banners. Military dances developed in these times, and through them soldiers trained to carry out timed actions that were coordinated to follow a set pattern. The same Han government bureau that collected folk music also recorded folk dances.

▶ This charming terra-cotta figure shows a lute player.

Note that the musician is kneeling, not sitting on a chair—this was typical in ancient China.

Other entertainments

Acrobats did balancing acts, walking on ropes stretched above the ground, as well as other tricks. People also enjoyed shows. Puppet masters used puppets to act out stories. One account dates puppet shows to 3,000 years ago.

In shadow puppet shows, an entertainer held up a wooden figure sculpted in human form. Light shining on the figure cast a shadow on a background, giving this form of theater its name.

The musician is wearing a hat or has an elaborate hairstyle.

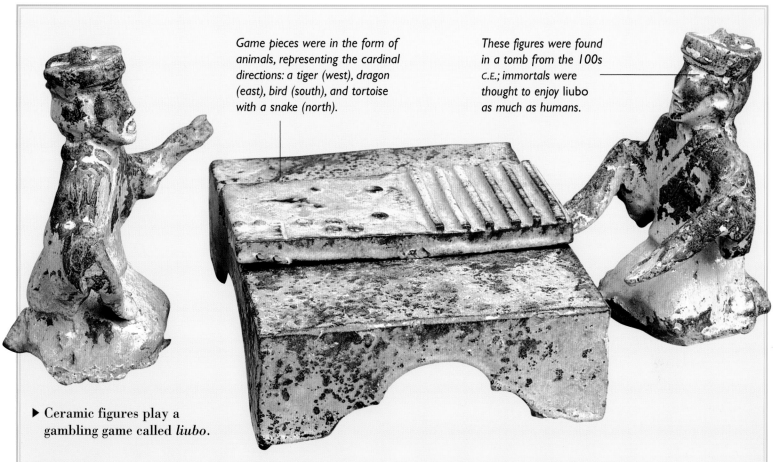

Game pieces were in the form of animals, representing the cardinal directions: a tiger (west), dragon (east), bird (south), and tortoise with a snake (north).

These figures were found in a tomb from the 100s C.E.; immortals were thought to enjoy liubo as much as humans.

▶ Ceramic figures play a gambling game called *liubo*.

Games

The Chinese enjoyed games as well. One popular game, called *yi* ("yee"), was a forerunner of the Japanese game known as *go*. In this game, players moved small playing pieces on a square board with criss-crossing squares. In some versions, the board has 17 vertical and horizontal lines. In others, there are 19 lines in each direction. One player had white pieces; the other played black. The aim was to control areas of the board and capture the opponent's pieces. An ancient text, written in the first 100 years C.E., links the game to Chinese **philosophy**: "The board must be square and represents the laws of Earth. The lines must be straight like the divine virtues. There are black and white stones, [equally] divided [like] **yin and yang**. Their arrangement on the board is like a model of the heavens."

Another popular pastime was a gambling game called *liubo* ("lee-oo-boh"). The rules for this game have not survived.

▼ The Chinese also had wind instruments. This unusual example was carved from a human thighbone.

The *qin*

The *qin* has strings stretched over a body that is long and slightly curved. Unlike a guitar or violin, it has no neck extending from the body. *Qin* have been found with anywhere from five to twenty-five strings. Paintings often show educated officials holding a *qin* as they sit in a beautiful landscape. Mastering the *qin* became one of the artistic talents expected of men of culture.

Beliefs and Philosophies

Like the ancient Egyptians, the ancient Chinese believed in life after death. They stocked the tombs of their rulers with many goods to ensure that they had everything they needed in the next life.

Life after death

In the earliest times, jade ornaments were commonly left in people's tombs. Two shapes in particular are often found—a small flat disk with a hole in it, called a *bi* ("bee"); and a long, hollow tube with squared sides, called a *cong* ("tsohng"). *Cong* are frequently decorated with designs that look like faces. Many burials have several dozen *bi* and *cong*. Scholars still debate the meaning of these shapes.

Zhou tombs are notable for their large number of **ritual** bronze vessels. These were intended to allow the dead to continue performing rituals in honor of their ancestors. Late Zhou burials have fewer ritual vessels and more objects from everyday life. Some tombs built for government officials contain piles of documents, including written lists of all the goods placed in the tomb. These lists help historians tremendously.

Han burials continued the shift toward everyday objects—tombs usually hold furniture, weapons, and musical instruments. Miniature models of structures and wall decorations reveal much about Han homes.

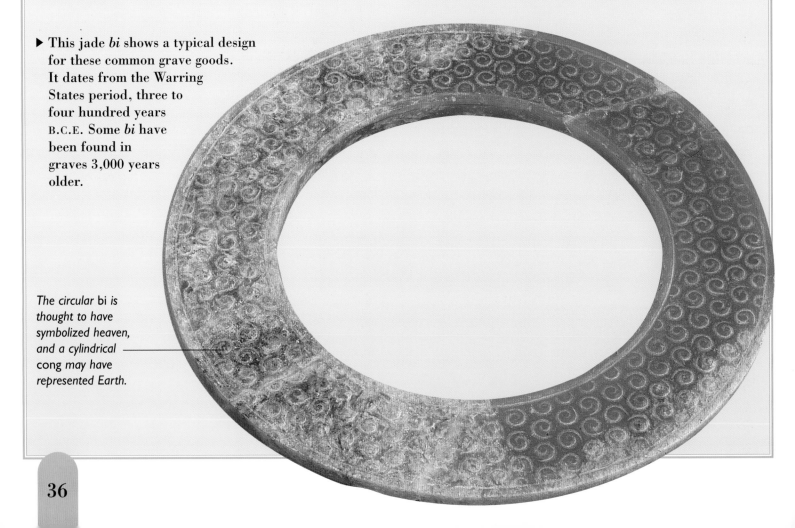

▶ This jade *bi* shows a typical design for these common grave goods. It dates from the Warring States period, three to four hundred years B.C.E. Some *bi* have been found in graves 3,000 years older.

The circular bi *is thought to have symbolized heaven, and a cylindrical cong may have represented Earth.*

Burial attendants

The burials of Shang rulers and nobles include the skeletons of loyal followers who were apparently supposed to attend to the needs of the spirit after death. (It is not known how willingly these attendants died.) A tomb from around 1200 B.C.E., probably for a Shang king, included 90 servants and several animals. Some Shang burials contained entire chariots, along with the horses needed to pull them.

Burial attendants still appear in Zhou times, but they are fewer in number. Although Qin Shi Huangdi's tomb is known for the thousands of terra-cotta soldiers and other attendants, it, too, has the skeletons of officials and servants.

Han tombs also hold the remains of attendants, though they have only a few. Small figures made of pottery, jade, wood, and metal are far more numerous. For instance, the tomb shared by Emperor Jingdi ("jeeng-dee") and his wife contains an impressive army of pottery soldiers. Unlike those of Qin Shi Huangdi, they are only about a third life-size, but they make a far larger army—numbering about 40,000.

Ritual sacrifice

Shang tombs also had people who were deliberately killed—victims of human sacrifice. The condition of their skeletons clearly distinguishes them from the attendants, since their heads are cleanly cut off. The skulls were buried in another part of the tomb. These sacrificed people were probably prisoners of war. Though attendants are found in burials from later periods, the practice of sacrifice disappeared after the Zhou rulers took power.

◀ This bronze lamp dates from the early Han period in the last two centuries B.C.E.

Openings in the cylinder allow light to shine through.

A handle can be turned to make an opening for placing a wick in the bottom of the cylinder.

The Chinese linked birds to the sun (and thus to light), making them perfect subjects for lamps.

Only the wealthy had lamps made of such expensive materials as bronze—most people had pottery lamps.

Burials

▶ These terra-cotta figures from Han times show a lively—and happy—group of musicians.

Burial attendants reflect all aspects of Chinese life—the military, the government, work, and even entertainment.

Most of the instruments have been broken off and lost, but this drummer still has his drum.

The size of these Han figures contrasts with the life-size army of Qin Shi Huangdi.

Burial practices did not remain the same over the many centuries of the ancient period. Along with changes in the goods placed in tombs and the presence or absence of attendants, the tombs themselves differed.

Changes over time

The earliest tombs were simply holes dug into the earth—deeper and larger if they were for rulers or wealthy people. Footholds were cut into the sides to allow workers to climb in and out while stocking the tomb with goods.

From around 1000 B.C.E., in Zhou times, the most powerful members of society had even larger tombs dug out of the earth. Sloping steps led to the center, where the body was placed.

The tomb of Qin Shi Huangdi, the first emperor of the Qin **dynasty**, was a huge complex covering 20 square miles (52 square kilometers). According to one ancient historian, the central burial mound once looked like a miniature version of the world, with some parts shaped like mountains and valleys. Mercury (a shiny, liquid metal) streamed down channels made to look like waterways, and stars were painted above. Around the burial chamber, **archaeologists** have discovered many pits, each containing a particular part of the household. For instance, a set of slaughtered horses and pottery figures appears in a "stable." Another section has the emperor's court attendants. Still other pits house the famous pottery army. Once the objects were in place, they were covered by wooden structures with tile roofs. Then the pits were filled in.

Han tomb builders carved their tombs out of rock, making caves. They also used brick and stone and built more elaborate structures. One tomb resembles a home, even including a bathroom.

The massive burial complexes of the kings and emperors took huge numbers of people a great deal of time—a measure of the emperors' power over their subjects. According to ancient reports, Qin Shi Huangdi ordered that construction should begin on his tomb soon after he took power. Eventually, the government passed laws specifying certain burial practices. One law limited the number of coffins a person could have, depending on his or her rank. Normally only top officials were allowed three. However, a burial from the Warring States period contains three for one lower-level official, who should have had only two.

▶ This burial suit was for a princess who died in the 100 years B.C.E.

Preserving the body

The Chinese never developed the skill in preserving dead bodies that the ancient Egyptians had. Still, they made many efforts to protect the deceased.

Jade symbolized eternal life and was thought to give protection from evil spirits and decay. For these reasons, jade objects were placed with bodies from early times. Later preparations became more complex. For instance, some members of the Han **imperial** family are buried in suits made of tiny jade plates. The bodies have since decayed, but archaeologists have reconstructed the suits to show how they originally fit.

In some royal burials, the thread was spun gold.

The suit is made of hundreds of jade plates attached by thread.

The head is laid on a bronze headrest.

It would probably have taken workers several years to make a suit like this, a clear indication of the huge resources commanded by noble families.

Two Leading Philosophies

Two important philosophers lived during Zhou times. Their teachings had tremendous influence on ancient China—and beyond. Confucius taught how people should behave in society. The writings of his followers became the core texts that men had to learn if they wanted to become scholar-officials. Laozi urged people to seek harmony with nature.

Confucianism

Confucius served the court of one local king, but when he felt that his advice was not followed, he left and began teaching. To him, a moral life meant fulfilling your role in society. Confucius saw society as having key relationships: ruler and subject, husband and wife, father and son, older and younger brothers, and friend to friend. Only friends could interact as equals. People of higher rank should not exploit or abuse those of lesser status. Each group had obligations to the other.

Those obligations extended to the family, a group Confucius saw as the basic unit of society. Fathers had the responsibility of raising and caring for their children. Sons had to show respect for their parents. Filial piety (honoring one's parents and one's ancestors) was the cornerstone of a strong, happy family.

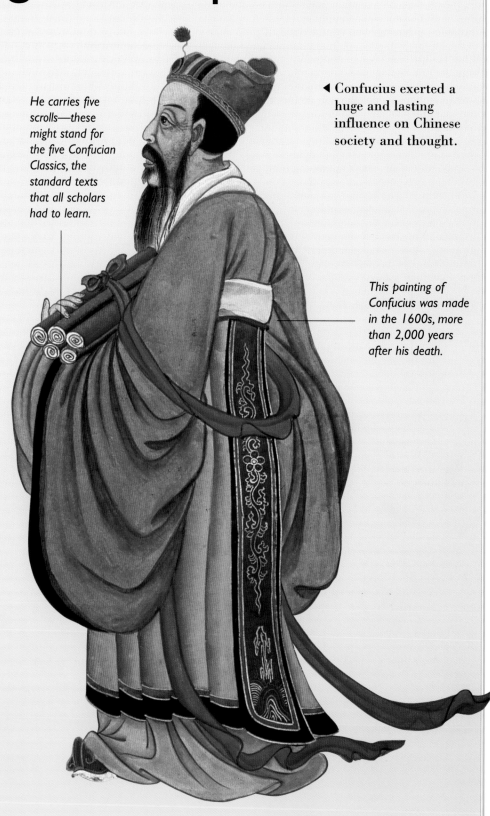

He carries five scrolls—these might stand for the five Confucian Classics, the standard texts that all scholars had to learn.

◀ Confucius exerted a huge and lasting influence on Chinese society and thought.

This painting of Confucius was made in the 1600s, more than 2,000 years after his death.

Confucianism had a deep influence on Chinese society. The emphasis on respect for parents shaped family relationships. His call for government based on morality was hardly followed at all times but did set a standard by which rulers could be judged. However, the emphasis on fathers and sons meant that women had a relatively weak position in society.

Daoism

Laozi lived about the same time as Confucius. He valued nature and its balance of forces. He did not think that human beings were the most important creatures on Earth. Indeed, he argued that humans could upset the natural order of the world.

Laozi's **philosophy** came to be called Daoism, or "the Way," and it had many followers. Daoism taught that action could be harmful. Inaction, or not doing, was more in keeping with the Way. In Laozi's view, the government should leave people alone. People, in turn, should stop envying their neighbors and striving to do more or to get more. Instead, they should be content with what they had, and try to live in harmony with the natural world.

▶ This bronze shows Laozi, the founder of Daoism, seated on a water buffalo. Daoism promoted becoming attuned with nature. Laozi seems to reflect that goal.

The Confucian Classics

Scholar-officials had to learn the five Confucian Classics. Qin Shi Huangdi, the first emperor, had ordered a massive book burning during his rule. When copies of the Classics were found later, the Han had the texts carved into stone to preserve them. In fact, some of the books had been written before Confucius had lived. The *Book of Documents* reflects Confucian advice on what makes good government. The *Book of Changes* (famous today as the *I Ching*) outlines the Chinese view of **yin** and **yang**.

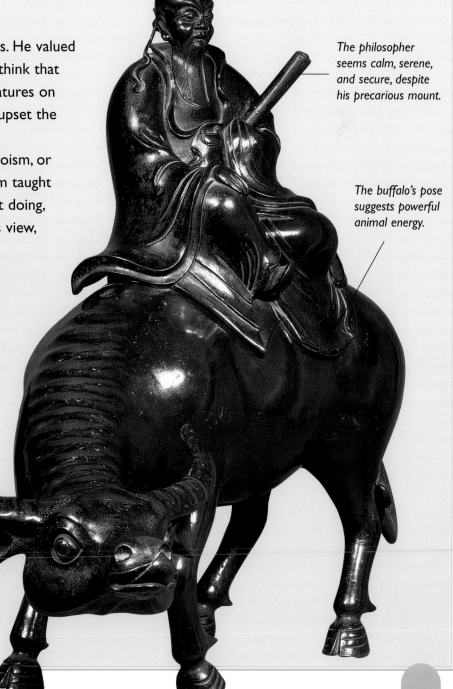

The philosopher seems calm, serene, and secure, despite his precarious mount.

The buffalo's pose suggests powerful animal energy.

New Ideas

Many ideas about heaven and the final destination of the human spirit took shape during Han times, some of them influenced by Daoism. Daoists adapted Chinese myths to illustrate their own **philosophy**. They also incorporated long-held beliefs, such as the ideas of *yin and yang*.

Judgement and heaven

Thinkers began to see a person's soul or spirit as having two parts. The lighter part rose to dwell in the clouds. The heavier part remained on Earth, around the person's grave. It was this part of the soul that needed food and other grave goods buried with the body. Failing to provide these goods endangered the living—a spirit that was not cared for could become angry and harass his or her relatives. Plus, by neglecting this obligation, the living were not carrying out their duty of filial piety.

Han thinkers also developed the idea of a judgement that took place after death. This became linked to a particular mountain in eastern China. There, the dead were judged and told whether or not their spirits would enjoy the blessings of heaven.

Some Daoists also claimed that people could become immortal. They said that people who did not die lived on an island off the eastern coast. Qin Shi Huangdi even sent an expedition in search of this place. Later, during the reign of Wudi, a Daoist thinker urged the emperor to make certain sacrifices that would allow him to gain immortality.

▼ Beautiful cave paintings dating from the 500s B.C.E. show the Queen Mother of the West and other heavenly spirits.

Temples at Dunhuang are full of Buddhist images, while caves there (including the one where this painting was found) were decorated with murals showing battles.

Mountains suggest the Queen Mother's origin as a mountain spirit.

Some of the spirits are riding birds—in some depictions, the Queen Mother of the West was shown as a bird.

▶ This ink drawing portrays the "Eight Daoist Immortals." These figures were worshiped by many in China in later centuries, showing the lasting impact of Daoism. Daoist temples had special halls dedicated to the Eight Immortals.

Believers worshiped at these temples during a spring festival and at other times of year.

The Eight Immortals represented different people—young and old, men and women, noble and common—who had all achieved wisdom by pursuing the Dao (or "the Way").

The Queen Mother

The Daoists also transformed a mythological figure, the Queen Mother of the West. She had been a mountain spirit but, under Daoism, she became the ruler of a blessed region of immortality. Belief in her increased, fuelling a popular movement that predicted the end of the **imperial** order and the creation of a new **empire**. This prophecy seemed to be fulfilled when Wang Mang ousted the Han ruler and took over the throne. Soon after, however, Han rule was restored.

Following the principle of *yin* and *yang*, with its emphasis on balance, the Queen Mother of the West was joined by another figure—the King Father of the East. A blessing from Han times, inscribed on a bronze mirror, read: "May you attain the highest political rank like the King Father of the East. May you attain longevity like the Queen Mother of the West."

Chinese coinage

The first material used as money in ancient China seems to have been cowrie shells. By the 400s B.C.E., various kingdoms were making bronze coins—some in the shape of knives or spades. When Qin Shi Huangdi established his empire, he created a standard coin that was round with a square hole in the center. These small copper coins could be strung together and carried easily. Han coins continued this design.

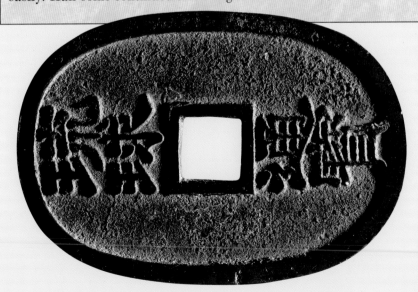

▲ Coins like this one were placed in tombs to provide money for the dead. Some coins were hung on treelike objects, decorated with symbols of the Queen Mother of the West.

Timeline

Note: many of the dates here are only approximate. Written records do not exist for some of these events.

8000 B.C.E.
farming begins in China

5000–3000 B.C.E.
Yangshao culture of north central China

3000–2200 B.C.E.
Longshan culture of northeast China

2000 B.C.E.
Chinese learn to make bronze

1600–1050 B.C.E.
Shang **dynasty**, the first dynasty to leave historical records, rules northern China

1200 B.C.E.
Shang dynasty adopts chariots from central Asia

Shang rulers begin using oracle bones to answer questions

c. 1050 B.C.E.
Zhou king overthrows Shang and establishes Zhou dynasty

771 B.C.E.
beginning of the Eastern Zhou period

551–479 B.C.E.
traditional dates for the life of Confucius

500s B.C.E.
probable period during which Laozi lived

400s B.C.E.
metal coins come into use in China

403–221 B.C.E.
prolonged fighting between competing rulers, called the Warring States period

300s B.C.E.
the *Laozi*, one of the basic books of Daoism, is written down

221 B.C.E.
Qin Shi Huangdi becomes first emperor of China

213 B.C.E.
Qin Shi Huangdi leads an expedition against the Xiongnu

210 B.C.E.
Qin Shi Huangdi dies; fighting breaks out

206 BC
Gaozu becomes emperor, launching the Han dynasty

166 B.C.E.
Xiongnu raid enters deep into China

141–87 B.C.E.
rule of Emperor Wudi, who expanded China and solidified the **civil service** system

139 B.C.E.
Wudi sends an official west, where he reaches Ferghana and sees the "Heavenly Horses"

111 B.C.E.
government takes over production of iron, salt, and alcohol

Han rule has extended by this time to present-day Korea and northern Vietnam

55 B.C.E.
Xiongnu splinter into several groups, reducing the threat they pose to China

1 C.E.
Chang'an, the Han capital, has population of nearly 250,000

2 C.E.
official government **census** puts population of Han China at about 60 million

9–23 C.E.
Wang Mang interrupts Han rule but is overthrown

25 C.E.
Emperor Guang Wudi restores Han dynasty

90–125 C.E.
Han rule enjoys last period of great power and prosperity

105 C.E.
traditional date Chinese give for invention of paper

220 C.E.
end of Han dynasty

Glossary

archaeologist person who finds, studies, and preserves the remains of ancient civilizations

artifact object made by people, such as a tool or weapon

cast form metal into a shape by pouring hot, liquid metal into a mold

cavalry soldiers who fight on horseback

census count of all the people in a land

civilization culture that reaches a high stage of development and includes an organized government, a belief system shared by all its people, a method of writing, different social classes, and an economic system that allows some people to do specialized work while others produce food

civil service group of scholar-officials who ran the Chinese imperial government

crossbow weapon that shoots a dart or short arrow; made by mounting a string on two pieces of wood fitted together in a cross shape

dynasty family or line of rulers who inherit power from each other

empire large lands or groups of lands ruled by one person or government

engraving design cut onto a surface

feudal system social system with wealthy landowners and rulers dominating society and peasants having little freedom

fire heat a pottery object at a high temperature in order to strengthen it

gilded coated with a thin layer of gold

imperial referring to the rule of an empire (a realm that includes many different peoples)

irrigation system for delivering water to dry land so that crops can grow

lacquer varnish made from the sap of a tree that grows in China; lacquer coating makes objects waterproof

longbow weapon that shoots arrows; made by fitting a long string to the top and bottom of a bent piece of wood

Mandate of Heaven Chinese idea that the gods would protect the rule of a just and virtuous king but allow an unjust one to be overthrown

mass-produce make goods in large quantities, as in a factory

nomad member of a group of people that roams from place to place, often to find fresh pasture for their herds of animals

philosophy system of beliefs or ideas about the world and people's place in it

post-and-lintel system method of building with vertical posts supporting horizontal lintels

regent adult who rules a kingdom or empire in the name of a child ruler

ritual special words and actions used to perform a ceremony, often religious in nature

Silk Road trade route used to carry silk and other goods from China to central Asia and Europe

technology ways of making objects or processing materials for people to use

tribute regular payment made by a weaker state to a stronger one

yin and yang principles in Chinese philosophy that represent the female (*yin*) and male (*yang*) forces; these are supposed to be in balance

zither stringed musical instrument with a flat back

Further Reading

Belloli, Andrea. *Exploring World Art*. Los Angeles: Getty Publications, 1999.

Cotterell, Arthur. *Ancient China*. New York: Dorling Kindersley, 2000.

Fields, Catherine. *China*. Chicago: Raintree, 2000.

Higgenbottom, Trevor. *China*. Chicago: Heinemann Library, 2000.

Immell, Myra. *The Han Dynasty*. Farmington Hills, Mich.: Gale Group, 2002.

Knight, Judson. *Ancient Civilizations*. Farmington Hills, Mich.: Gale Group, 2000.

Patent, Dorothy Hinshaw. *The Incredible Story of China's Buried Warriors*. Tarrytown, N.Y.: Marshall Cavendish, 2000.

Sherman, Josepha. *Your Travel Guide to Ancient China*. Minneapolis, Minn.: Lerner Publishing, 2003.

Shuter, Jane. *Ancient Chinese Art*. Chicago: Heinemann Library, 2001.

Steele, Philip. *Ancient China*. New York: Anness Publishing, 2002.

Tull, Mary, Tristan Franklin, and Cynthia Black. *Northern Asia: Understanding Geography and History Through Art*. Chicago: Raintree, 2000.

Uecker, Jeffry. *History Through Art Timeline*. Worcester, Mass.: Davis Publishers, 2001.

Woods, Mary B., and Michael Woods. *Ancient Construction*. Minneapolis, Minn.: Lerner Publishing, 2000.

Index